THE LIFE & TIMES OF MICHIGAN

A Smile-Infested Tour of a Great Great Lakes State

Harry and Nancy Knitter

© Copyright 1999 Harry W. Knitter

THE LIFE & RHYMES OF MICHIGAN

Copyright © 1999 by Harry Knitter

All rights reserved. No part of this book may be reproduced or transmitted in any form or by any means, electronic or mechanical, including photocopying, recording, or by any information storage and retrieval system, without permission in writing from the publisher.

Published by Kordene Publications, Ltd.
P.O. Box 636, Clarkston, Michigan 48347-0636

Publisher's Cataloging-in-Publication Data

Knitter, Harry W. and Nancy C.
The Life & Rhymes of Michigan / A Smile-Infested Tour of a Great
Great Lakes State / Harry and Nancy Knitter — Clarkston, Michigan:
Kordene Publications, Ltd., © 1999

        p.   ill.   cm.

ISBN 0-9652333-3-2

1. Travel   2. Poetry   3. Humor

Printed in the United States of America

Contents

About the Authors

Harry and Nancy Knitter have traveled to many corners of the world on business and occasionally for pleasure. Harry has been a writer and marketing executive for more than 35 years. He's written scripts, speeches, press releases, catalog and ad copy for several major corporations, including Chrysler and FTD.

In 1996, he wrote his first book, *HOLDING PATTERN: Airport Waiting Made Easy*. Two additional travel books followed:

Why You Should Take Your Travel Agent to Lunch,

and

101 Stupid Things Business Travelers Do to Sabotage Success.

He also wrote a book of prose and poetry on flowers called *A Sweet Sampling of Floral Delights*, with contributions from Nancy.

He has been a free-lance writer, a theater critic for his hometown newspaper, and — in his spare time — he plays the piano at parties, at local dining establishments, and for his own amusement.

Nancy has taught reading skills to youngsters for years and is now retired and teaching reading to her grandkids. She's also writing fine prose and poetry and has had both published. She has traveled extensively and has participated significantly in the formation of Kordene Publications, of which she is a vice-president.

The Knitters have three sons and two grandchildren, and they live in southeast Michigan.

This book is dedicated
to the memory
of a close friend and native Michigander,
Doug Hagemann,
and the
Hagemann family.

Introduction

This is a book of poetry with a little bit of prose mixed in, and it's designed to give you a view of Michigan you may never have experienced.

As you turn the pages, you will be embarking on a pleasurable journey through a great Great Lakes state, our home state of Michigan. However, we want to forewarn you that this is anything but a travelogue. For example, you shouldn't expect that all of our descriptions of destinations will be geographically, demographically, or scientifically accurate. But they are fun to read, and we know you'll be comfortable taking them with a grain of salt, since we wrote them with tongues-in-cheek. Metaphorically, we're already neck deep in swamp muck.

As you proceed up the sunrise shore, you'll sense that our perspective on Michigan is just a bit off-beat, as are many of our fellow Michiganders. But our view is that a sense of humor is one of the most important ingredients to happiness, and we are not comfortable among curmudgeons or grouches. If you like to frown a lot, you're reading the wrong book.

Now, finally, a bit of general information about Michigan.

Right at the start, you'll notice that we're different than other states since we have two — not one, but two — peninsulas to keep track of. A bridge connects the two parts, but that doesn't necessarily mean that we act like one state. On the contrary, we have those "Yoopers" up north doing their thing and the rest of the Michiganders from the Lower Peninsula doing another.

We are a diverse state that produces everything from sugar beets to flowers, cherries to Chevrolets. We also produce more than our expected share of outstanding scholars and achievers, musicians, artists, and writers.

Michigan borders on four of the five Great Lakes, creating a shore line of 1,700 miles where tourists can throw empty beer cans. But we're smart enough to include a deposit on beverage containers, so we pocket the dime when a visitor chucks a beer can on our beaches.

Michigan is 384 miles long and 233 miles wide, and is larger in total area than Connecticut, Delaware, Massachusetts, and Rhode Island combined. Because of all the water that surrounds us, our state has the highest per capita boat ownership of any other state in the country. So there are millions of fishermen and water skiers around these parts, as well as golfers, snow skiers, hikers, bikers, and campers.

We've written about many of the attractions of our state in this book. But the best way to experience our state is to come across the state line and explore our natural beauty, our growing cities, and our peaceful countrysides.

We need your tourist dollars. Welcome to Michigan. And...

Life in Michigan:
From Boblo to Faygo

Anyone who has spent time as a resident of Michigan knows that there are certain names and words that trigger the recollection of vivid memories of a past that seemed more friendly and less challenging than our lifestyle of today.

Boblo Island, for example, creates visions of carefree, warm summer days, picnic lunches on checkered table cloths, and time spent aboard the paddle-wheel boats that chugged from the mainland many times each day in season. Before or after the trip, kids and adults quenched their thirsts with Faygo soda, featuring everyone's favorite flavor, "Red Pop."

If Red Pop wasn't available, Vernor's Ginger Ale soda was a welcome substitute with a large majority of its distribution in Michigan.

A variety of musical groups performed on the island, perfecting their acts before they unveiled them to more sophisticated audiences.

Of course, there are other names and images that bring back pleasant memories of life in Michigan, including:

Downtown Hudson's
Belle Isle Casino
Chesaning Showboat
Pewabic Pottery
Stroh's Beer
Sanders Ice Cream
and Hot Chocolate Sauce
The Fisher Building

Van Patrick

WJR Radio with J.P. McCarthy,
Bud Guest, Karl Haas, Mike Whorf,
Fat Bob Taylor, and others

Travel information from Michigan
AAA with Len Barnes

Greenfield Village and the
Henry Ford Museum

Bobby Layne

The Nederlanders

The Fords, Iacoccas, Knudsens,
Coles, and other stalwarts of the
automotive industry

Olympia

Michigan and Trumbull

Jerry Cavanaugh

George Romney

Eastern Market

The Free Press Marathon

Opening Day

Joe Schmidt

Belle Isle

Doak Walker

"Soapy" Williams

Today's Names of Note

These are some of the people who have made Michigan a
Great Great Lakes State:

John Engler, Governor
Michelle Engler
The Triplets
Dennis Archer
Barry Sanders
Ernie Harwell
Bob Talbert
Joe Falls
Al Kaline
The Howe Family
Grant Hill
Mort Crim
Rick Inatome
Carmen Harlan
Heinz Prechter
The Ilitch Family
Chuck Forbes
Don & Jerrietta Milton
Bob Eaton
Isaiah Thomas
Joe Dumars
Steve Yzerman
Mitch Albom
Frank Kelley
Bo Schembechler
Bishop Kenneth Povish

Gwen Frostic
Len Barnes
David DiChiera
Michael Behan
David Newman
Jim Harper
Dick Purtan
David Sowerby
Ron Davies
Larry Parrish
Jerry Lewis
Mike Whorf
Neeme Järvi
Scotty Bowman
Paul W. Smith
Pete Waldmeir
The Gaylords
Soupy Sales
Dr. Jessie J. Fry
Mother Waddles
Prof. Linda Peckham
Jeff Daniels
Joe Meur
Lloyd Carr
Dr. Dan White
Jim and Barb Pryor

Part One:
ALONG THE SUNRISE SHORES

Sunrise

It's as dark as the inside of a hollow pumpkin.
And as quiet as a chapel at midnight.
I feel a breeze and hear the wishy-washy water
wishing and washing
on the stone-covered beach.
It's dark and no one can see nuthin'.

Suddenly, magically, a glow appears —
a gradual glow, slow and low.
On the horizon, a slit. A very simple, slight slit.
Now the glow stretches out to the shore.
The slit becomes less slight.
And as the water shimmers,
we see the glimmer of light.

The glow emerges. It's unstoppable.
It spreads and the sky appears
as if a slide from a giant projector.
Shimmering ripples below, clouds above.
Now comes the sun.

Like the yoke of an egg,
It spills out on the horizon,
forming a golden half circle that
casts an orange tint on the sky.

Now we can see birds,
swooping to the water and gliding in the wind.
And a fishing boat coming close to shore.
It's still and quiet.

Sunrise.
The birth of another day.

Getting Started

Our bags are packed, we're on our way
We've waited anxiously for this day.
Let's hope that we won't later find
We've left something important behind.

The kids — already notorious snackers —
Are munching mouthfuls of crispy crackers.
But we don't mind all that infernal chewing
As long as that's *all* they wind up doing.

The car is full of fuel and ready to go
Unless there's something about it we don't know.
Our first stop will be many miles ahead
By that time we'll all be tired and ready for bed.

We enjoy spending time together
And we hope for exceptional weather
In two weeks, we'll finish our roaming
Anxious for a little "homing."
At last, we'll return and then
Start planning the next time we'll depart
once again.

The State Line

This wonderful state of mine
has no visible, nor easily discernible state line.
There's simply nothing to define
My state's (a great state) state line.

Was it by someone's grand design
That no one actually marked
our state line?
How can *anything* be perfectly fine
When we can't find the bleeping state line?

Summon the gov., the mayor, and the
sheriff by nine
Someone has come in and pilfered
Our precious state line.
It's vanished like a brown paper bag
Of cheap red wine.
With our state spreading in all directions
This situation is a big concern of mine.

Now, the whole thing may seem trivial
and not at all convivial
But I'm sure you'll agree
That some kind of border
Would be very much in order.

So I'll start to count to nine
…please, *someone*, return our state line,
So we can once more feel dandy and fine.

Motown Is No Town

...Without warm-hearted
optimists who open their arms
to strangers and open their billfolds
to those in need.

...without cheerleaders who
make the world aware of the
positive change underway
in a city with ambitions to be great once more.

...without honest leaders who
promise citizens to
create positive improvements
and deliver on their promises.

...without those who
consider skin color
incidental
inconsequential
and
insignificant.

...without those who would
hope for a better day
for a great city.

Detroit Is on the Rise.

A Pothole Is No Picnic

If you should see a pothole
On any Michigan road
We hope you'll steer clear of it
Or you'll wind up being towed.

Potholes were invented by the devil
To rattle the teeth, shake the kidneys,
and flatten the tire.
After you have encountered
his cruel creation,
It's a lot less difficult
to live in the land of fire.

He thrives on sending us
into a total rage
When we find our
car disabled
So we cuss and swear
and lose our cool
And our trip to heaven
is indefinitely tabled.

So don't let the miserable pothole
spoil your day
Just be sure you drive around it
and let someone else pay.

Hamtramck

It will always be a mystery to me
How the city of Hamtramck came to be
Right in the center of mighty Motown
And full of Poles who work hard, play hard,
and rarely frown.

They love to cook, bake, and eat all day
With ox tails, pig tails, and Czarniña
prepared the old country way.
And each year before the start of Lent
They bake paczki's with jelly inside
and a treat that's heaven sent.

They're fun-loving people with lots of spirit
But I have a tough question
and some may fear it:

I want to know
how the city grew with another around it

When they let down their guard,
Detroit moved in to surround it.

Clarkston

The downtown donut shop is a daily stop
Since we have made Clarkston, Mich. our home,
By munching our donuts, we're less inclined to roam.
(That's why we have written this friendly tome.)

We live in a beautiful town
surrounded by lakes
And we enjoy all this beauty
Without any snakes or quakes.

We like its friendliness and wholesome spirit
And feel its charm whenever we're near it.
It's a Yankee Doodle type of town
Where people tend to smile more than they tend to frown.

They support high school sports
Summer concerts, parades, and rich cherry tortes.
And when you move here from another place
You're not a stranger, but a friendly face.

I guess you can tell we're happy here
And we'll enjoy Clarkston for years to come,
that's clear.

A Capital Idea

There's something special about Lansing
That inspires spirited celebration and dancing.
Perhaps, in truth, it has something to do
With the capital view
That elected terms be limited to a measly two.

Politicians would have us believe
They'll serve their time and then leave.
But we know better — or should we say worse —
When they turn up as well-paid lobbyists
Oh, what a dastardly curse!

They roam the capitol aisles in search of old cronies,
Invite them to lunch and the track full of ponies
Wine and dine both true friends and the phonies
And feed them sales pitches full of balonies.

I think we can say that it's the American way
To lobby for what we believe should be done.
So join me in roasting those who are coasting
After they experienced their day in the sun.

We hope they all exhibit a sense of humor
And don't treat our ribbing like an unwanted tumor.
To be in politics, one must be thick of skin
And not take too seriously the world we're in.

By the Way...

Saginaw is an Indian name that originated with the Sauk Indians that inhabited the area hundreds of years ago. Later, the Chippewa tribe was also prominent in the region. Fur trading and lumbering were the major commercial enterprises of the 1800s, with lumbering reaching its peak in the 1890s. Today, the city of Saginaw and its surrounding towns are tied to many other major industries, including automotive, chemicals, aluminum, grey iron, and fertilizers.

Saginaw county is agricultural, though residential and commercial development moves are taking a bite out of the available land. Recreational sports abound in the Saginaw area, with fishing, hunting, and boating among the most popular. There are almost 500 miles of streams and rivers to delight fishermen.

Nearby Frankenmuth offers Bavarian ambiance and unique shopping opportunities at the Christmas shops and specialty stores that line the streets.

Chicken dinners at Zehnder's and The Bavarian Inn provide tourists with delightful dining year-round.

Bronner's Christmas store is stocked with colorful and high-quality holiday decorations from many corners of the world.

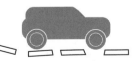

Gimme More Saginaw, Grampaw!

When you've been to Saginaw,
It's not what you've done that counts
But what you saw.

Some think it takes more than views
Or blues or queues or ewes
Or huge pots of mom's beef stews
to make the news.

It's the **views** we can't afford to lose
If we do, pity those in our shoes
For the lake displays the blues
And fishermen come in three's and two's.

These outdoors gals and guys
Realize that it's their eyes
That get the prize
When they take time to
See the views
In Saginaw U.S. of A.
Where people come to play
Every day
In the Bay.

Michigan
Places and Events
to Discover

Tapawingo Gourmet Dining in Ellsworth

Golden Mushroom Restaurant in Southfield

Lelli's on Woodward for Italian Food

Windsor, Looking West at the Detroit Skyline

MIS

Tiger Stadium

Joe Louis Arena

Fireworks at Hart Plaza

Cobo Hall During the International Auto Show

The Grand Prix

Woodward Avenue

Birmingham Downtown

Meadowbrook

Concours d'Elegance

Potato Festival in Posen

Orchestra Hall

The Somerset Collection

Around the Grand Piano
at Border's Books and Music, Birmingham

The Ren Cen

The Model Train Exhibit in Holly

Greektown

Any Jazz Club Featuring Buddy Budson

Montreux Jazz Festival
Charlevoix Art Festival
Salmon Festival in Rogers City
Pike Street in Pontiac with Greg Nichols
The DIA
Michigan State's Jazz Band I Concerts
A Lugnuts Home Game in Lansing
The Collage Concerts at Hill Auditorium
Football at the Big House
Saturday Morning Soccer with Kayla
The Bridge Walk at Mackinac
Port Huron to Mackinac Sailboat Competition
"Friday Night Live" in Traverse City
Silver Bells in Lansing
"High Tea" at the Holly Hotel in Holly
Doughnuts on Main Street in Clarkston
The Auto Show at Northwood
Sunset at Shanty Creek
The Peach Festival in Romeo
Picnics at Belle Isle
Baker's Keyboard Lounge
"Friday Night Live" at Uncle Buck's, Lake Orion

Part Two:
ON OUR WAY UP NORTH

Frankenmuth

Visitors come from far and near
To enjoy Bronner's holiday cheer.
For right here, Christmas comes
Every day of the year.

There's plenty to savor
With a Bavarian flavor
Like succulent chicken dinners
That make us all feel like winners.

Tourists come here to play,
Enjoy music and dancing the Old World way
Polkas and waltzes with a lively beat
And food that is always a gastronomical treat.

Shops display gifts from many nations
To take home or send to friends and relations
This is a town where visitor satisfaction
Is often Frankenmuth's main attraction.

The Thumb

Michigan's uncrowded Thumb is the place to see
When everyone else is where everyone else should be.
In the Thumb, beautiful sunrises on Lake Huron are routine
With sailboats and fishing boats
Floating in every picturesque scene.

Traffic is lighter on this side of the state
With less people, and more fish to fill your plate.
Tourists find the scenery and enjoy open spaces
The Thumb is one of the best vacation places.

If you go elsewhere, your brain must be numb
'Cause for true relaxation, you should head for The Thumb.
But don't think about buying a home down by the bay.
We love you as tourists, but we hope you won't stay.

For it doesn't take degrees from a local college
To realize that if everyone buys a local cottage
The Thumb would become
Like other places.
Expensive, overcrowded, and full of
rush hour faces.

Port Austin

It's easy to get lost in
The pretty little city of Port Austin
Especially if you happen to be
From the big city like Boston.

It's on the Huron lake shore
Where there are surprises in store
For residents and tourists alike
Who travel by car, bike, or just hike.

There are fish to be caught
In hot spots that are eagerly sought
Your fishlines are often taut
The fish taste much better than those
that are bought.

You'll never be bothered by crowded roads
But by local critters like frogs and toads.
And don't ever worry what all this is costin'
For life is priceless here in Port Austin.

Live on 75

You begin your trip in Toledo,
One eye on the road and one on the speedo.
Point your car north and soon you're in Motown
Workin' through traffic, and gettin' it down.
No jive, man, you're alive on 75.

North of town, you don't have to go far
Before you see the famous Pentastar
Where the German influence is so pervasive
And Daimler folks are now so persuasive.

Now you're close to Flint
And you manage to catch just one more glint
Of the car building factories that are large
Where once they built cars, they now meet in bars
Remember the prosperous days gone by
And try not to think of the scars.
No jive, man, you're alive on 75.

You pass West Branch, where the discount stores
Make you forget all the chores.
Winds are turning cooler,
Feels like someone opened the fridge.
We must be nearing the north country,
And soon we'll be crossing the bridge.

We've traversed the lower peninsula end to end
And we've run plum out of freeway.

Au Revoir, my friend.

Summer
Up North

Surf's up — slurping, sloshing,
Neighbors watching,
"o-my-goshing."

Gotta come back here,
momma.

Faraway horizon splits
Our postcard picture in two:
On top, the placid sky
foreshadows a picturesque sunset;
Below, the churning, wind-whipped
surf, white-capped waves, are wild and
wonderfully wet.

Gotta come back here,
momma.

Counting ships and tanker trips
Crossing right to left, left to right
Night and day, dark to light.

Make a wish for a fresh-caught fish
Soon to become a tasty dish.

Gotta come back here,
momma.

Tomatoes red with runny juice
Sweet-tart berries and deep red cherries
Mobile tinkles in the cool, crisp breeze
Hummingbird flits about with ease.

Gotta come back here,
momma.

Leaf tips turning colors here
Gonna paint the forest early this year.
Listen to the surf spank the ragged beach
Fishin' boats far out of reach.

Gotta come back here,
momma.

Life's not fair, but I don't care
When I get a Whiff
Of that unpolluted air.

Water's rough and fishin's tough
Can't never get enough
Of Summer Up North.

Gotta come back here, momma.
Gotta come back here.

By the Way...

Breathtaking scenery along the Lake Huron shore,
Calcite freighters motoring along the horizon,
historic lighthouses, and plentiful fishing are
all evident features of Rogers City and its
neighboring communities.
With a large contingent of Polish residents,
excellent ethnic food stores, sausage and bakery
shops are within easy reach to satisfy
the heartiest appetites.
A focal point of the freighter
activity is the world's largest limestone
quarry, located in Rogers City.
One of the most beautiful parks
in the statewide system is Hoeft State Park,
just north of the city.
At dawn each morning,
the sun rises over Lake Huron,
often providing glorious sunrises
on days without cloud cover.
Long stretches of uncrowded beaches
invite visitors to stroll in the sand
and discover smooth, water-washed stones
and aged gray driftwood
that often winds up on a tourist's
shelf or desk back home.

Where's Roger?

Roy never rode Trigger here,
Maris never poked a long one over the fence.
And Richard never tried to compose a Broadway ditty
About the little town called Rogers City.

In our state, there are names of some towns
that inspire both smiles and frowns
Like Bravo, Muttonville, Climax, Maybee, Colon, Crisp,
Dreamland, Paw Paw, Ralph, and Hell
But what bothers me, as you can tell,
Is: **who put the Roger in Rogers City?**
(A town without an apostrophe.)

There must have been a Roger involved
When the city was named. If so, the
mystery can be expeditiously solved.

But I'm betting that ol' Roger
May have been a smart old codger
Who lived in these parts for a while,
Impressed the locals with his style,
Gave the city his name
And before they caught up with his game
Moved to California
To pursue fortune and fame.

Though you could easily claim,
exclaim or disclaim
The thesis I've proposed
I'll stand corrected and admit my shame
(the case is closed)
When you realize that I'm pulling your leg
'Cause that's *my* game.

The Simple Game of Golf

Out of the woods
And out of the farm land
The rolling hills and valleys
have been freed of crops and horses
And now our state is known for its
Spectacular golf courses.
The swingers take to the links
With everything but their
kitchen sinks
But they never seem to
improve the score,
and they go on
swinging and hollering "fore."

They ride in the fanciest of carts
When they should be walking
for the good of their hearts.

Most golfers play for fun
Until they shoot a hole in one.
And then
They party
Eat Hearty
Talk Smarty.

But I find golf
To be enlightening,
For as if I were
struck by a bolt of lightning,
I realize it's not the game
that is important,
or even the score.

What is significant
is that I'm allowed to fail...
and still come back for more.

Gotta Have One More Bite

Fudge.
Chocolate sludge.
You be the judge.
We'll hold no grudge.

Chewy.
Gooey.
Uncle Louie's
acting screwy.
He ate too much
With dates, with nuts and such.
His stomach's full of fudge
And the sludge refuses to budge.

Now he's lost his crutch.
Should have tightened his clutch.

Hooray! He located the crutch
On granny's favorite hutch.
Thank you very much.
Keep in touch!

By the way...

Traverse City is known as the Cherry Capital of the world,
and visitors must be prepared to encounter
a wide variety of products originating from cherries,
including sausage and burgers.
Traverse City is located at the foot of Grand Traverse Bay
and features both naturally beautiful
vistas and an exceptional array of tourist attractions.
One of the most pleasant drives in the area
will take you out to Old Mission at the end of a long,
thin peninsula that juts out into Grand Traverse Bay.
You'll pass cherry orchards and wineries
with sampling rooms along the way.
Among the most popular activities
in the Traverse City area are boating, sailing, golf,
and listening to a variety of music
on warm summer evenings at nearby
Interlochen Music Camp.

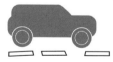

Trouble in Traverse City

There's Trouble in Traverse City
And it's not so neat and pretty.
That's TROUBLE — With a capital "T"
and it ends with "E" and that spells TROUBLE.

It's a micro-brewin' in Traverse City.
The hillcrest folks are condescending,
Looking down on bayfront folks and pretending
That just because of their lofty status
They'll never have to look straight at us.

On the bay, way down below, the well-heeled motel-owning citizens know
That the hillcrest wealth is just for show.
And the bayfront crowd is happy as can be
When they can look up to the hills and shout,
"NO VACANCY!"

By now, we hope you know this is a ruse
So crack a smile and put away the noose.
T.C. is always a great place to be
And the residents work in full harmony.

Stay there and you'll see.

By the Way...

*Interlochen is the home of the
Interlochen Center for the Arts and a
National Music Camp.*

*The world-renowned fine arts center
offers instruction in music, visual arts,
theater and dance.
In addition, world-class
performers visit during the summer months.*

*Interlochen is a small town surrounded by
lakes and woodlands.
And the growing population from
Traverse City.*

Could Interlochen Rock 'n' Sock?

The birds in the trees
Whistle sweet melodies
But some of the young musicians
Treat the music like helodies.

One summer week
(This is tongue-in-cheek)
There were some sounds made here
That should have stayed here.

When they found they had leaked out,
the camp counselors just freaked out.

And Interlochen
Started Rockin' and Sockin'.

To report that the music was loud and sour
Would make everyone dour.
Let's just say it was loud
And rattled the eardrums of the disgruntled crowd.

The drummers tried to beat it
Doctors began to treat it
Wal-Mart offered to greet it
Hackers tried to delete it.

But nothing worked, and the music perked
And Interlochen rocked and socked,
happily ever after.

The Moment of Truth

Here I am, perched precariously
at the top of the hill
My bony knees are knocking (I need a strong pill).
There's no turning back, I've got to go down.
If I don't ski to the bottom, they'll think I'm a clown.

My skis are waxed, my pants skin tight
My goggles are frosted, I've lost my sight.
Skiing is dangerous, as you may know,
So I've lost my desire
(I'd much rather be sprawled
in front of a fire).

I see myself rocketing into the nearest tree
And a long hospital stay in the future for me.
I'm about to start a collection of broken bones
And I'm going to need some substantial loans.

They say skiing in Michigan is the thing to do
But I'd rather stand here and enjoy the great view.
These goggles make me look like someone named SVEN.
Here we go!
I'm on my way at the count of **ten**.

One

One-point-five...

One and 13/16...

Downstaters

Some know them as the "fudgies"
And others are downright "curmudgies"
But northerners' greatest delight
Is one that has launched many a fight.

That's when they feel their taters
And boldly label us downstaters.

We bring money that makes them able
To put bread and butter on their table
But they earn nothin' but rotten tomaters
When they label us "them darned downstaters."

We bring action and life to northern Mich
But we'd like to express our fondest wish
You can have our best skiers and skaters
If you'll only stop calling us "downstaters."

Part Three:
WE'VE ARRIVED IN YOOPERVILLE

By the Way...

The city of Marquette is the largest
community in the Upper Peninsula
of Michigan. Iron ore is the area's
primary industry, and Great Lakes freighters
make frequent appearances at the docks.
Other industries contributing to the
area economy include mining, lumbering,
farming, and tourism.
Visitors from the Lower Peninsula
and other locations enjoy fishing
and water sports on over 1,800 lakes and
ponds in Marquette county, and soak up the scenery
along 78 miles of Lake Superior shoreline,
and in state and national forests.
Winter sports lovers enjoy skiing,
snowmobiling, and ice fishing.
Marquette is the home of
Northern Michigan University.

Going to Marquette

Everyone knows how c-c-c-c-cold it will get
As soon as someone mentions winter
in shivery Marquette.
And when icicles form let's not forget
That there's also a summer in sunny Marquette.

It occurs between the first of July
and the Fifth
When thousands of tourists pack up and
head north.
They always enjoy the celebration and never regret
Spending summer each year in sunny Marquette.

Why summer is so short
no one really knows
But on the fifth of July
They begin to prepare for snows.

Perhaps old man winter would frown and fret
If they wouldn't let him come early
To s-s-s-unny Marquette.

So Who Laughs Last?

Anyone living in Michigan knows
That some hotheads practically come to blows
Over the division in our state so unique
It is debated week after week after week.
Oh, what anguish we wreak!

The argument is ridiculous, an utter and complete joke
When the Loopers* deride the Yoopers**
Implying the U.P. is full of country bumpkins
Who do little but fish, hunt, and carve their pumpkins.

Then, when the Loopers put aside their sophistication,
They head to the U.P. for summer vacation
And what do they do with their precious time?
They hunt, fish, and buy beanies in Engadine.

Before long, though, they pack up again
Drive south across the bridge and then
Act as though they're brilliant and rich
But in their hearts they have an itch to switch.

They know Da Yoopers have it made
Hiking in the sun and snoozing in the shade.
And when it's time to relax and take things slow,
Da Yoopers stay where they are,
Raking in the Loopers sophisticated dough.

* Lower peninsula residents

** Upper peninsula residents

55

By the Way...

*Copper Harbor, Michigan's northernmost community,
offers visitors a variety of recreational
activities, including snowmobiling and skiing
in the winter
and deep sea fishing, scuba diving, and boating
in the summer.
Development of the area began in 1843
after discovery of large copper deposits.
Plan to visit Isle Royale, a national park
in Lake Superior, and be sure you don't
miss the Copper Harbor lighthouse built
in 1867. The combination of extraordinary
natural beauty along with historic landmarks
draws downstaters and out-of-staters
to Copper Harbor during the peak travel season
each summer.*

Copper Harbor

They all come here and congregate.
A few relate, some procrastinate,
and others relocate.
They're the retirees of police
and sheriffs' departments
Who move to Copper Harbor
and buy luxury apartments.

They arrive from Detroit, Lansing,
and Traverse City
Armed with pensions, badges and nitty-gritty.
Whether on horseback or in squad cars,
they love the view here
But to be honest,
they find little to do here.

Soon they get tired of the lawful
And start to search for crooks
who are awful.
So back to the city they go,
their spouses protesting,
But now they find their lives
much more arresting.

Should the Sioux Sue the Soo?

Many years ago, the

tribe of Indians lived in
the region now known as

St. Marie.

The locks in Sault St. Marie are called

Locks.

What happened to

Sioux?

Sue, I say.

Or should I have said
Sioux?

Or possibly
Sault?

Oh foo.
I'm through.

You, too?

By the Way...

Mackinac Island, the third oldest
settlement in Michigan, operates at
a distinctly slower pace,
partly because no motorized vehicles
are allowed. The primary modes
of transportation, then, are bicycles
and horse-drawn carriages.
Visitors can access the island
by boat from St. Ignace
or Mackinaw City on the mainland.
Mackinac Island is a mecca
for shopping, golf, sightseeing,
and boating, but many of the incoming visitors
head for the fudge counters of local
stores, where they will find
some of the finest fudge concocted anywhere.
Lovely old homes, mansions, and hotels
designed in Victorian themes take
tourists back to the early days of
the century. In a more recent period,
the movie Somewhere in Time was
filmed on the island.

Mackinac Island

High above the straits so blue and foamy
We fly to the island, hospitable and homey.
There's the majestic Grand, with its long, long porch
And to the south we see the lake called Torch.

No cars allowed, so islanders walk briskly
Between points of interest on foot or horse.
Or pedal a bike if you're so inclined
And view magnificent beauty only nature designed.

Visit the Grand for an afternoon tea
Or chat with sailors before they head out to sea.
The ferry boat does its hourly chore
Taking visitors away and bringing still more.

Life on the island is calm and quiet
Some summer soon, you ought to try it.
Leave everything at home,
And be prepared to roam.

This is a lifestyle that's so relaxing
You never think of issues difficult, complex, or taxing.
When you're here, get in the mood for good food.
And as for manners,
islanders are never rude, crude, or lewd.

Come join them, dude.

Part Four:
DOWN THE SUNSET SHORE

Harbor Springs Eternal

The memory lasts
Of sails and masts
Spinnakers puffed
Sailbags stuffed.

Dining spots bustling
Waitresses hustling
Shoppers spending
Summer's ending.

Tourists leaving
Shopkeepers grieving
Seeing is believing
Parking spots available.

Leaves are falling
Winter's calling
Children bawling
Room rates appalling.

Next year save your money,
So you can take me there, honey.

By the Way...

Petoskey, a lovely resort town on a bluff overlooking Little Traverse Bay, boasts of being a summer hangout for the late Ernest Hemingway, who wrote several of his early short stories while vacationing in the area. Quaint shops and art galleries abound in the historic gaslight district in downtown Petoskey. Superior restaurants on the Bay offer placid views of sailboats and beautiful sunsets.

Getting there is also an experience of beauty as you wind your way along the shoreline of Lake Michigan.

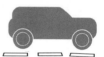

Petoskey

Petoskey is a picturesque place to reside
If you like hills, gorgeous views, and community pride.
For the folks who live here don't tolerate
The ugly, you see, like
Litter, empty bottles, or the golden arches of Mickey D.

The views of Lake Michigan are simply spectacular
Or "cool," as described in the northern vernacular.
Sailboats float by as if on a blue cloud,
Navigating silently and avoiding the crowd.

When it's time to pack up and head south
Petoskey visitors feel down in the mouth.
Because they know that as far as they can see
Where they're going rates secondarily.

Petoskey and Charlevoix make a great pair
And now Bay Harbor is located there.
For extraordinary fun, you have a perfect right to be
In the middle of summer in spectacular Petoskey.

By the Way...

*Charlevoix is a charming community of historical homes
and neighborhoods established by vacationing downstaters
as well as by many returning vacationers from various parts
of the U.S. Strips along the city's curbs are planted
with colorful petunias throughout the growing season.
Charlevoix is a jewel on Lake Michigan
with beautiful beaches and scenic shorelines.
In addition, the city is located on the western shore
of Lake Charlevoix, the third largest inland lake in Michigan.
The availability of fresh fish is boundless. Bring a cooler
and go to John Cross Fisheries for fresh-caught whitefish
and several varieties of smoked fish throughout the summer.
In the center of town, luxurious yachts, power boats,
and sailboats keep the bridge tender busy as traffic
comes to a halt every half hour to allow the boats
to pass from the one lake to the other.
Winter is a slower paced time of the year;
many shops and restaurants are closed,
but several nearby resorts offer skiing,
both cross-country and downhill.*

Charlevoix

Unconventional dwellings constructed of stone
Are found in Charlevoix, Michigan alone
Surrounded by water, this
Postcard-worthy town
Is populated by homes
Of architectural renown.

With boutiques unique
And planked walks that creak,
Charlevoix is a tourist's paradise
That demands
To be seen,
Not once,
But twice.

Boat crews amble down Main street
Hoping to find a dining treat.
Some walk the length of town
Accompanied by petunias all around.

If you ever get to see this place,
Smiles will form on your sunburned face.
Here, even traffic moves at a leisurely pace
And life is simply a leisurely stroll...
with nary a trace of a race.

By the Way...

Grand Rapids is the second largest city in Michigan,
located 144 miles northwest of Detroit.
Originally settled by Dutch immigrants,
it is the most conservative part of the state.
For many years, Grand Rapids was considered
a center for furniture manufacturing;
however, the economy is much more diversified
at the present time.
Convention facilities in the downtown area
draw many visitors to the city to enjoy
a wide variety of attractions,
including the Gerald A. Ford Presidential Museum
on the Grand River, museums, theaters,
good restaurants, and shopping.
Other appealing tourist stops include the
John Ball Zoological Park and the
Frederik Meijer Gardens.

Grand Rapids

If you've never visited G.R., you really
ought to do it
The Grand River slices right through it.
You can stand here and feel Lake Michigan's breezes
And catch cold when Lansing sneezes.

Grand Rapids is a clean and solid town
That perks you up when you're feelin' down.
Their population in the state may be number two
But the area is tops for things to do.

With Meijer, Amway, and other firms
Headquartering here on favorable terms,
Grand Rapids is a working city
Whose people are charming and friendly,
And the girls are pretty.

The Gerald Ford Museum is a great attraction
But if you're looking for livelier action,
There's golf on many nearby courses
Where formerly there were cows and horses.

Sleeping Bear Dunes

Visitors travel from many faraway foreign lands
To feel the grains of sand sift through their
foreign hands
Study the Sleeping Bear's legendary lore
And listen to the slumbering mythical bear snore.

Scale the steep shifting sandy mountain
(Wish we were close to a water fountain).
With our climb,
We view the Lake Michigan shore
And then we vow to return once more.

Sand follows us back to our home
Happens every time we get here as we roam.
We take beach stones home as treasure.
But memories
beat souvenirs by any measure.

So come and visit the mighty bear
But prepare for him to be elsewhere.

Part Five:
IN THE HOME STRETCH

By the Way...

*Holland was founded by Dutch immigrants
in 1847 and is close to the shores of
Lake Michigan. In the spring, millions of
tulips are in bloom during the annual
Holland Tulip Festival. A 225-year-old windmill
and the wooden shoe factory are among the many
Dutch-themed shops and restaurants found in the area.
Holland is a biker's paradise with 100 miles of trails,
some along Lake Michigan.
Resort towns of Saugatuck and Douglas are
within minutes south of Holland, MI.*

A Taste of Europe

They click up their heels in Holland, Michigan, USA,
Where thousands come to play each May.
It's a town where they don't sing the blues
Unless they find termites in their wooden shoes.

Few windmills swat the air around here
And there are no canals or narrow homes.
There is no flower auction or van Gogh collection
But the natives enjoy the displays of Dutch heritage and
time to do some reflection.

When the warm weather comes
And the friendly tourist bus hums
Local merchants realize mighty sums
Of dollars from tulips, not mums.

Dutch Treat

Nothing will ever be exactly the same
After love ignites a lifelong flame
And tulips touch ever so romantically.

Days go by and we go on living;
and soon we find ourselves forgiving.
And tulips touch ever so gently.

Love comes our way in daily ration
Expressed with happiness
and passion.
And tulips touch ever so warmly.

I was so sad, and often lonely
Then you became my one and only…
As tulips touched ever so reassuringly.

The love we give,
The words we say
Will never leave
Or drift away.

When tulips touch ever so faithfully.

Sweetheart, our love will blossom
like the delicate petals of a beautiful flower.

— Harry Knitter
from *A Sweet Sampling of Floral Delights*

YAWWWWW-N-N-nnnnn

I'm sitting in my car,
staring at the map.
And wondering whether
I could sneak in some time
to take a nap.
The weather's threatening
And we're due for a cold, cold snap.
The time is ripe,
I'll need no hype,
Could you please take the rap
So I could take a nap?

I'm pondering the significance
of the generation gap.
Oops! I spilled my coffee
into the middle of my lap.
Now I've got to get to the cleaners
Without creating a major flap.
(Wonder if I should ignore the stain
And just take a much-needed nap?)

Turn on any music except the noise they call rap.
I'm eager, I'm ready, and I'm going
to take a nap.

The Great Lakes

While other states would opt for more,
Michigan has the most Great Lakes shore.
And sometimes others may feel inferior
When we show off our beautiful Superior.

Lake Huron offers surprises galore
And each morning we peek to see what's in store
Lake Michigan provides some beautiful bays
And sunsets to conclude our sunshiny days.

But let's not forget one more
Now don't get teary...
Let us sing the praises of old Lake Erie
Once thought to be dead
But the report was premature, it is said.

It's unfortunate that our Great Lakes scenario
Can't include the great Lake Ontario
But let's not ourselves be greedy
When Torontonians plainly are so much
more needy.

Saugatuck

We're bluebloods all the way, on holiday
Sipping tea in our B & B by the bay.
We'd never be caught dead
in a blue-collar truck
We're the BMW
B & B
crowd of Saugatuck.

We arrive about five with our bags
by Gucci.
After we change, we're always ready
for some hootchy
and some kootchy.
Then we amble along wobbly wooden docks
and put aside our calendars and clocks.

But soon it's time to leave and bid adieu
After one last glimpse of the bay so blue
We've displayed ourselves in the latest fashions
And managed to exercise some of our energies and passions.

So we climb into our Beemer sedans
With the tops down, we can exhibit our blueblood tans
We're delighted to be so full of good luck
When we motor down to sunny Saugatuck.

By the Way...

*St. Joseph is a beautiful town
on the Lake Michigan shore,
next door to Benton Harbor.*

*It's a pleasant trip from Indiana, from the
Chicago area, or from any part of Michigan.*

*St. Joseph is the home of the St. Joseph
historic lighthouse and catwalk.
The lighthouse is one of the first
two such structures to be built on
Lake Michigan.*

Meet Moe
From the Town of St. Joe

In the town of St. Joe,
there lived a muscular young man named
Moe...
A shy and quiet sort of mellow fellow
Until one day (pull up a chair and stay)
Moe dropped a 50-pound brick on his toe.

Now Moe is just — well, just so-so
After the painful and damaging
blow to his toe.

He may try to deny it
But he's resumed being quiet

And won't talk to no one no mo.

What's All That Noise in Kalamazoo?

If you're not a "hummer,"
Pity — it's a bloody bummer.
For we "hummers" — ages 12 to 92 —
Are off to kazoo in K'zoo.

You can learn it in a minute
(It's much easier than a Spinet)
You get out what you put in it
But sometimes…
It sounds like a cat when you skin it.

You hum — don't ever blow it.
If you're lousy, the world will know it.
When you're not playing,
It's easy to stow it.
You never have to tow it.
When you're off to kazoo in
Kalamazoo.

It's Over

And though it seems our poetic
journey is over;
What's next, you ask?
We have a large unfinished task.

There's always another frontier, dear friends,
Before our supply of rhyming words ends.

Unless our rhymes are
thought to be soft and drippy,
we'd like to take a crack
at Louisiana and Mississippi.

But my real inclination is this:
To pause for a deep breath
And an encouraging kiss.

We'll recharge our energy,
Hit a few strokes,
Tell one or two jokes,
Then visit the blokes
In Shakespeare's U.K.
And write another book
In an Elizabethan way.

Wherefore art thou, Marvin?

Sun Sets

Another day comes to an end
Another long summer day,
departing like a short-term friend.

We hardly had time to get to know ye
There are so many things we'd like to show ye.

But we know you have to go.
To spread your golden rays on other days.
To light up the sky and shimmer on the water.

But there you are, fading into our memory.
You bring us warmth, but you don't last.
One moment you're there,
And then you've gone away.

To spread your golden rays
On another day.

Part Six:
TRAVEL PLANNING INFORMATION

For Information...

On Bicycling

Michigan Bicycle Touring
3512 Red School Road
Kingsley, MI 49649
616-263-5885
www.bikembt.com

On Boat Charters

Charter Boat Assn.
P.O. Box 80323
Lansing, MI 48908
800-MCBA-971

On Canoeing

Recreational Canoeing Assn.
P.O. Box 357
Baldwin, MI 49304
616-745-1554

On Casinos

Travel Michigan
P.O. Box 3393
Livonia, MI 48151
888-78GREAT

On C.C. Skiing

Travel Michigan
(see above)

Great Lakes Nordic Ski Council
P.O. Box 525
Suttons Bay, MI 49682
616-271-6314
www.skinordic.org

On Downhill Skiing

Travel Michigan
(see above)

On Festivals, etc.	**Michigan Festivals & Events Assn.** P.O. Box 22 Chesaning, MI 48616 517-845-2080
On Hunting & Fishing	**Michigan DNR** License Control Div. P.O. Box 30181 Lansing, MI 48090 517-373-1204
On Golf	**800-GOLF-MI**
On Lodging	**Mich. Hotel, Motel, and Resort Assn.** 6105 W. St. Joseph Lansing, MI 48917 517-323-1818 800-772-9988 www.michiganhotels.org
	Michigan Lake to Lake B & B Assn. 3143 Logan Valley Rd. Traverse City, MI 49684

Resorts of All Sorts

You can't lose
When you choose
To lengthen your fuse
And jettison the blues
At one of Michigan's resorts
For indoor and outdoor sports

Shanty Creek
Bellaire

Crystal Mountain
Benzie County

Boyne Mountain Resort
Boyne Falls

McGuire's Resort
Cadillac

Woodmoor Resort
Drummond Island

Treetops Sylvan Resort
Gaylord

Hidden Valley
Gaylord

Marsh Ridge
Gaylord

Thunder Bay Golf Resort
Hillman

Sugar Loaf
Leelanau County

Garland
Lewiston

Lakewood Shores
Oscoda

Bed and Breakfast Stops

You're in for some special treats if you decide to book your overnight stay in one of Michigan's many excellent Bed and Breakfast facilities. Here are some of the finest:

Torch Lake B & B
Alden
616-331-6424

Linda's Lighthouse Inn
Algonac
810-794-2292

Castle in the Country
Allegan
888-673-8054

The Artful Lodger
Ann Arbor
734-769-0653

Grand Victorian
Bellaire
800-545-0780

Chicago Street Inn
Brooklyn
517-592-3888

Bridge Street Inn
Charlevoix
616-547-2804

Millpond Inn
Clarkston
248-620-6520

House on the Hill
Ellsworth
616-588-6304

Locust Manor
Farmington Hills
248-471-2278

Bavarian Town B & B
Frankenmuth
517-652-8057

Boyden House B & B
Grand Haven
616-846-3538

Windy Ridge B & B
Harbor Springs
800-409-4095

The Buck Stop
Hiawatha Forest
906-446-3360

Holly Crossing
Holly
800-556-2262

Interlochen Aire
Interlochen
616-276-6941

Stuart Avenue Inn
Kalamazoo
616-342-0230

The Indian Wood
Lake Orion
248-693-2257

Haan's 1830 Inn
Mackinac Island
906-847-6244

The National House Inn
Marshall
6161-781-7274

Cottage on the Bay
Michigamme
906-323-6191

San Souci Euro Inn
New Buffalo
616-756-3141

The Hexagon House
Pentwater
616-869-4102

Serenity
Petoskey
616-347-6171

Paint Creek B & B
Rochester Hills
248-651-6785

Hess Manor
Romeo
810-752-4726

Newnham SunCatcher Inn
Saugatuck
616-857-4249

Red Dog B & B
Saugatuck
616-857-8851

Morning Glory Beach
Suttons Bay
616-271-6047

The Grainery B & B
Traverse City
616-946-8325

For a complete listing, send $4.00 for postage and handling to:

Michigan B & B Directory
3143 Logan Valley Road
Traverse City, MI 49684

Part Seven:
KORDENE TRAVEL BOOKS

Makes Time Fly
When Your Plane Doesn't

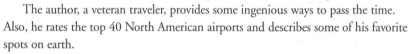

HOLDING PATTERN:
Airport Waiting Made Easy
by Harry Knitter

Why be discouraged, demoralized, and disappointed when you have to wait for your next flight? This Kordene book will make your waiting time fun and interesting.

The author, a veteran traveler, provides some ingenious ways to pass the time. Also, he rates the top 40 North American airports and describes some of his favorite spots on earth.

$9.95 plus $3.50 S & H
Call 888-567-3363

The Book to Read Before You Book

Why You Should Take
Your Travel Agent to Lunch
by Harry Knitter

Your best ally when traveling is your travel agent. The author suggests ways to find a good one, and describes how to capitalize on their knowledge and experience.

He tells why you should avoid booking on the computer and describes several interesting trips he took to Europe. Collaborator William Chiles provides valuable travel agent background.

$9.95 plus $3.50 S & H
Call 888-567-3363

The Book to Save Time and Money While Traveling

101 Stupid Things Business Travelers Do to Sabotage Success
by Harry Knitter

Million-mile traveler and author Harry Knitter tells how to avoid problems and added costs while traveling. Sometimes it just means avoiding an unnecessary trip.

Young businesspeople will find this book an easy way to make trips more productive.

$9.95 plus $3.50 for S & H
Call 888-567-3363

The Flower Book Even Florists Like to Read

A Sweet Sampling of Floral Delights
by Harry Knitter

This is an ideal book for get-well giving, anniversaries, or any special occasions. In prose and poetry, the author covers flower-giving from many perspectives, most of them humorous.

He also includes stories about florists delivering flowers.

$7.95 plus $3.50 for S & H
Call 888-567-3363

ORDER FORM

To order additional copies of this book or any other Kordene Publications book (titles below), send your name and shipping address along with a check for the amount of your purchase to: Kordene Publications, P.O. Box 636, Clarkston, MI 48347-0636.

Author: Harry Knitter

Name _____

Shipping Address _____

City _____ State _____ Zip _____

Book Titles	Price	Quantity
1. *The Life & Rhymes of Michigan*	$8.95	_____
2. *HOLDING PATTERN: Airport Waiting Made Easy*	$9.95	_____
3. *Why You Should Take Your Travel Agent to Lunch*	$9.95	_____
4. *101 Stupid Things Business Travelers Do to Sabotage Success*	$9.95	_____
5. *A Sweet Sampling of Floral Delights*	$7.95	_____

Shipping and handling charges (send check with order and save shipping and handling charges):
• $3.50 for one book
• $4.00 for two or three books
• $1.00 each, for orders of four or more books

Michigan residents add 6% sales tax.